# Contents

- 8    **CHAPTER 1: Peter Parker is Spider-Man!**
- 10   Introducing Peter Parker
- 12   Peter's family and friends
- 14   Peter's Spidey suits
- 16   Peter's Spidey gear
- 18   Spider-Man: Avenger!
- 20   Peter's Spider Lair
- 22   *The Daily Bugle*

- 24   **CHAPTER 2: Other Spider-Heroes**
- 26   Miles Morales is Spider-Man!
- 28   Gwen Stacy is Ghost-Spider!
- 30   Anya Corazon is Spider-Girl!
- 32   Ben Reilly is Scarlet Spider!
- 34   A Spidey for every Universe!
- 36   Spideys united!

- 38   **CHAPTER 3: The Villains in Spidey's Web**
- 40   Spidey vs. Green Goblin
- 42   Spidey vs. Doctor Octopus
- 44   Spidey vs. Venom
- 46   Spidey vs. Mysterio
- 48   Spidey vs. Sandman
- 50   Spidey vs. Vulture
- 52   Spidey vs. Electro
- 54   Spidey vs. Rhino

- 56   Glossary
- 58   Index
- 60   Acknowledgments

# Getting to know THE MULTIVERSE

Being a Spider-Hero can be complicated. You learn a lot on your adventures, including the fact that the world you live in is **not the only one**! Science and magic can open doors to **other versions of Planet Earth**—where some things are just like your own reality, and others are **completely different**. This collection of **parallel worlds** is known as **the Multiverse**. In this book, you will meet some of its amazing **heroes** and **villains**!

### Blue boxes

Throughout the book, there are blue boxes, like this one, and pages with a blue background. These are here to let you know that a LEGO® set shows a storyline from the Marvel Cinematic Universe (MCU). If you don't see a blue box or the page isn't blue, the LEGO® Marvel set is not from one of the movies.

### Blue pages

Here is an example of the blue background that features on pages showing LEGO sets from the MCU.

Marvel Cinematic Universe

# Introducing Peter Parker

Everyone knows the web-slinging Super Hero, Spider-Man. The sight of his red-and-blue suit is enough to send most crooks running for cover. Underneath the mask is a super-smart teenager named Peter Parker. He got his powers when he was bitten by a spider.

**SPIDER-MAN**

### Peter Parker

Peter likes to live a normal, everyday life when he can. But he's always ready to swing into action!

**MASKED CROOKS**

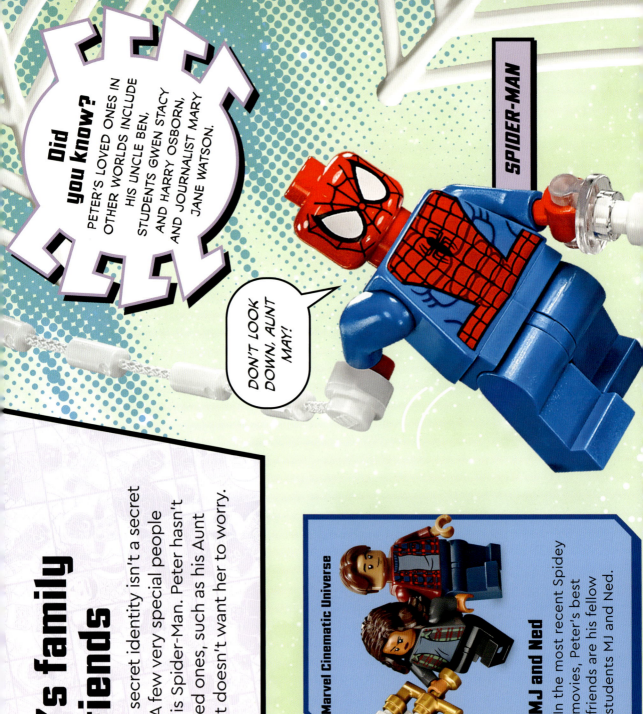

## Did you know?
PETER'S LOVED ONES IN OTHER WORLDS INCLUDE HIS UNCLE BEN, STUDENTS GWEN STACY AND HARRY OSBORN, AND JOURNALIST MARY JANE WATSON.

**SPIDER-MAN**

"DON'T LOOK DOWN, AUNT MAY!"

## Peter's family and friends

Peter Parker's secret identity isn't a secret to everyone! A few very special people know that he is Spider-Man. Peter hasn't told other loved ones, such as his Aunt May. Peter just doesn't want her to worry.

**Marvel Cinematic Universe**

**MJ and Ned**
In the most recent Spidey movies, Peter's best friends are his fellow students MJ and Ned.

# Peter's Spidey suits

Soon after he got his super-powers, Peter designed and made his first crime-fighting suit. He wore a mask to hide his true identity and invented a way to shoot webs from his wrists. Now he has lots of suits to choose from, all packed with awesome spider-tech.

**Cyborg suit**
When Spidey was injured, a fellow scientist upgraded his suit with cyborg tech.

**Stealth suit**
Spidey's stealth suit deflects light away from his body, making him invisible.

PETER'S IRON SPIDER SUIT WAS MADE BY **IRON MAN** TONY STARK!

**Did you know?**
PETER'S IRON SPIDER SUIT HAS CAMERAS IN THE TIPS OF ITS EXTRA LEGS. THIS MEANS THAT HE CAN SEE AROUND CORNERS!

# Peter's Spidey gear

Sometimes it takes more than super-powers to save the day. That's why Peter loves inventing tough new tech to give him an edge against his enemies. From giant robot spiders to supersonic jets, there's nothing Peter can't put together and pilot like a pro!

I LOVE A GOOD WALK!

SPIDER-MAN

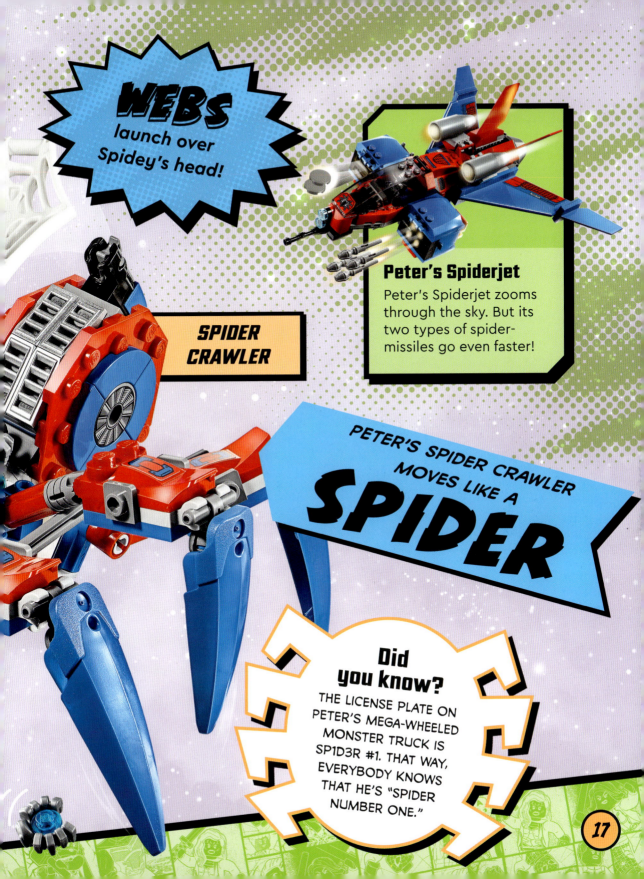

**WEBS** launch over Spidey's head!

### Peter's Spiderjet
Peter's Spiderjet zooms through the sky. But its two types of spider-missiles go even faster!

**SPIDER CRAWLER**

PETER'S SPIDER CRAWLER MOVES LIKE A **SPIDER**

### Did you know?
THE LICENSE PLATE ON PETER'S MEGA-WHEELED MONSTER TRUCK IS SP1D3R #1. THAT WAY, EVERYBODY KNOWS THAT HE'S "SPIDER NUMBER ONE."

Marvel Cinematic Universe

# Spider-Man: Avenger!

As the world's most famous Super Hero team, the Avengers just had to have Spider-Man as a member. Iron Man was the first to see young Peter's potential. Before long, Spidey was slinging webs alongside Black Widow, Captain America, Thor, and more!

**Did you know?** TONY STARK IS A GREAT INVENTOR AS WELL AS A SUPER HERO, JUST LIKE PETER. NO WONDER THEY GET ALONG SO WELL.

"*TEAMWORK* makes the dream work!"

THOR

CAPTAIN AMERICA

# Peter's Spider Lair

Every Super Hero needs a base, and Spider-Man's might just be the coolest of them all. The Spider Lair has a supercomputer for tracking villains, tools for making awesome tech, and a launchpad for a Spider-Bike. It also has a skate ramp and a basketball hoop!

**Locked up**
Not even the Green Goblin can escape from the Spider Lair's jail cell.

SPIDEY SUITS FOR EVERY OCCASION

## The Daily Bugle

When Peter isn't fighting crime he takes photos for *The Daily Bugle*. The famous news source has a huge New York office and plenty of stories happen on its doorstep. Still, no one there knows how Peter's pictures get quite so close to the action!

### Did you know?
Peter sets up cameras with motion sensors to take pictures of himself in action as Spider-Man. Selling them helps pay his bills.

### J. Jonah Jameson
The Bugle is run by J. Jonah Jameson. He likes Peter Parker but can't stand Spidey!

**FIRESTAR**

**GHOST-SPIDER**

**SPIDER-MAN**

**DOC OCK**

*I LOVE BREAKING NEWS!*

# Chapter 2
# Other Spider-Heroes

PETER ISN'T THE ONLY ONE WITH SPIDER-POWERS. ALL KINDS OF AWESOME WEB WARRIORS HELP HIM KEEP THE MULTIVERSE SAFE.

# Miles Morales is Spider-Man!

Miles was still at school when a spider bite gave him special powers. He didn't want to be a Super Hero, but he stepped up to be Spider-Man when Peter Parker disappeared. He soon got into the swing of things, and now shares the Spidey name with Peter.

**Miles Morales**
Earth defense agency S.H.I.E.L.D. made Miles's red-and-black spider suit just for him.

**CARNAGE**

### Did you know?
THE SPIDER THAT BIT MILES CAME FROM A LAB WHERE SCIENTISTS WERE TRYING TO RECREATE PETER PARKER'S SPIDER-POWERS!

# Gwen Stacy is Ghost-Spider!

Gwen and Peter are pals in many different universes. In at least one, it was Gwen, not Peter, who became a Super Hero thanks to a spider's bite. When this version of Gwen travels to our world, she becomes Ghost-Spider to do her good deeds!

"I'm a goodie in a HOODIE!"

**Gwen Stacy**
Gwen's hobbies include skateboarding, drumming in a band, and visiting different universes.

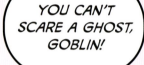

YOU CAN'T SCARE A GHOST, GOBLIN!

GHOST-SPIDER

# Anya Corazon is Spider-Girl!

When this high school student saved a sorcerer's life, he gave her spider-powers! As a Super Hero, she is best known as Spider-Girl, but sometimes calls herself Araña (the Spanish word for spider). She has teamed up with many other web-slingers, including Peter Parker.

HANDS UP, DOC OCK!

SPIDER-GIRL

**Anya Corazon**
Anya has a great sense of humor. Her half-mask reveals a cheeky grin.

"My spider TATTOO lets me know when danger is near!"

# Ben Reilly is Scarlet Spider!

A shady scientist made this exact copy of Peter in a lab. He was designed to be an enemy for Spider-Man, but the two of them teamed up instead! To help people tell the pair apart, Ben now fights crime as the Scarlet Spider.

**Ben Reilly**
Ben bought his blue spider hoodie from a spider-themed gift shop!

**Did you know?**
BEN NAMED HIMSELF AFTER PETER'S UNCLE BEN AND AUNT MAY. MAY'S SURNAME WAS REILLY BEFORE SHE GOT MARRIED.

"I keep my face masked to protect **PETER'S** identity!"

# A Spidey for every Universe!

Peter is amazed to learn that there are many different versions of planet Earth, each with its own Spider-Heroes. Some are very similar to our own Peter, while others are very different!

**SPIDER-MAN NOIR**

On one Earth, it is still the 1930s and the only colors are shades of gray. This world's Peter Parker is a detective as well as a Super Hero.

**SPIDER-MAN 2099**

Miguel O'Hara comes from a futuristic Earth where it is already the year 2099. He used advanced science to give himself spider-powers.

**INDESTRUCTIBLE** suit cannot be torn!

## MASK MADE FROM PILOT'S GOGGLES

### SPIDER-HAM

*I'm the only real spider here!*

Peter Porker might be the strangest Spider-Hero of them all. He started life as an ordinary spider, then got bitten by a radioactive pig!

**Marvel Cinematic Universe**

### ZOMBIE HUNTER SPIDEY

In a world full of zombies, it helps to have magic on your side! This version of Peter gets his by wearing Doctor Strange's Cloak of Levitation.

35

**Marvel Cinematic Universe**

# Spideys united!

Peter had his work cut out when a magic spell sucked villains from across the Multiverse into his home city. Luckily, two more Peters came along for the ride. They joined forces for an epic showdown on top of New York's Statue of Liberty!

### NED LEEDS

**BLACK-AND-GOLD SUIT HELPS PRIME SPIDEY STAND OUT!**

**Did you know?**
IN REAL LIFE, THE STATUE OF LIBERTY IS GREEN. IN THE MARVEL CINEMATIC UNIVERSE, IT'S BEEN RESTORED TO ITS ORIGINAL COPPER COLOR.

### GREEN GOBLIN

"My pals are the best in the **MULTIVERSE!**"

### Three Peters
These three Peters are all great heroes, but each has lived a very different life.

# Chapter 3
# The Villains in Spidey's Web

YOU CAN JUDGE A SUPER HERO BY THE QUALITY OF HIS ENEMIES, AND SPIDEY HAS DONE BATTLE WITH THE BEST OF THE WORST!

# Spidey vs. Green Goblin

As a child, Norman Osborn had nightmares about a gruesome goblin. As an adult, he decided to become that goblin! Now he lives a double life, posing as a law-abiding businessman by day and doing everything he can to destroy Spider-Man by night.

"I love **HALLOWEEN** but I can't stand spiders!"

I'M MEAN AND GREEN!

### Did you know?
A SECRET FORMULA GIVES THE GOBLIN SUPER-STRENGTH AND MAKES HIM SUPER-CUNNING. IT DOESN'T TURN HIM GREEN, THOUGH. THAT'S JUST A SCARY DISGUISE!

**GREEN GOBLIN**

MECH SUIT MADE BY NORMAN'S COMPANY, **OSCORP**

## DOC OCK

### Did you know?
DOC OCK'S REAL NAME IS OTTO OCTAVIUS. HE WAS A FAMOUS SCIENTIST BEFORE HE TURNED TO A LIFE OF CRIME.

### Mind control
Doctor Octopus controls his metal arms with his mind. He can make them move even when he's not wearing them!

### Different Doc
In the Marvel Spidey and His Amazing Friends universe, Doc Ock is a young female scientist called Olivia Octavius.

*"I'M BAD, BUT I GIVE GOOD HUGS"*

43

## Spidey vs. Venom

Spidey's strangest foe is a black, gooey blob from another planet. When it couldn't take over Peter's mind and body, it bonded with another human host to become a warped version of the web-slinger. Venom is now the sworn enemy of every Spider-Hero.

**MILES MORALES SPIDER-MAN**

THIS IS NOT A BONDING EXERCISE!

FAKE SPIDEY MASK, BUT REAL **FANGS!**

**VENOM**

### Pork Grind
When Venom bonds with Multiverse hero Spider-Ham, he pigs out as Pork Grind!

# Spidey vs. Mysterio

Spidey can't believe his eyes when he faces this master of illusion. Mysterio has no super-powers, just a suit full of special effects. He uses holograms, smoke machines, and other tricks to confuse his enemies and to make the world think Spider-Man is a villain!

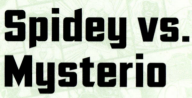

*MY TECH TRICKS ARE THE TOPS!*

**MYSTERIO**

### Did you know?
MYSTERIO'S REAL NAME IS QUENTIN BECK. HE LEARNED THE SECRETS OF SPECIAL EFFECTS WHILE WORKING ON HOLLYWOOD MOVIES.

*"REALITY is whatever I say it is!"*

Marvel Cinematic Universe

# Spidey vs. Sandman

Fighting Flint Marko is no day at the beach. This crook can turn himself into sand, slipping through his opponents' fingers or becoming a rock-hard block of concrete. He can become any shape or size, and even fly in the form of a sandstorm.

**LIZARD**

**SPIDER-MAN**

"Let me shake you by the **SAND!**"

HOW'D YOU GET SO BIG?

**Did you know?** SANDMAN GOT HIS POWERS WHEN HE GOT TOO CLOSE TO A DANGEROUS SCIENCE EXPERIMENT.

MARKO CAN LOOK LIKE A MAN OR A **MONSTER!**

Marvel Cinematic Universe

# Spidey vs. Vulture

The sky's no limit when the Vulture hatches his plans! He flies like a bird on giant wings and takes what he wants like a thieving magpie.

**IRON MAN**

WINGS MADE FROM SALVAGED AND **STOLEN TECH**

### Unmasked
Several villains have worn the Vulture gear, but the most frequent flyer is a man called Adrian Toomes. In his comic-book adventures, Toomes is too proud to wear a mask!

### Did you know?
ON THE BIG SCREEN, TOOMES TEAMS UP WITH SHOCKER TO STEAL TOP-SECRET TECH FROM TONY STARK AND THE OTHER AVENGERS.

# Spidey vs. Electro

Spider-Man is in for a shock every time he encounters Electro. An electrical accident turned mild-mannered Max Dillon into a high-voltage villain. Now he is hungry for power! The more he absorbs, the more he can blast out, in the form of lightning bolts.

"If power corrupts, I'm guilty as **CHARGED!**"

TIME TO MAKE A FORK IN THE ROAD!

BODY GLOWS **BLUE** WITH ELECTRICAL ENERGY!

ELECTRO

# Spidey vs. Rhino

Some of Spidey's foes have super-smarts on their side. Others, like Aleksei Sytsevich, are all about brute force. Gamma radiation gave him Hulk-like strength, and a rhinoceros battle suit boosts his powers further. Now Aleksei crashes from crime to crime as the hard-headed Rhino.

### Rhino Suits
Some Rhino suits are smaller than others, but all are super-tough. This one is from a LEGO Marvel Spidey and His Amazing Friends set.

"You won't get **UNDER MY SKIN** Spider-Man!"

HAHA! THAT TICKLES!

HERE COMES THE WRECKING BALL!

RHINO

HUGE HORNED HEAD HIDES THE REAL ALEKSEI

SPIDER-MAN

**Did you know?** IN SOME REALITIES, THE VILLAIN KNOWN AS THE RHINO DOESN'T JUST WEAR A RHINOCEROS SUIT. HE ACTUALLY TURNS INTO ONE!

# Glossary

**Avenger**
Someone who strikes back against wrongs done to them or others.

**Encounter**
A meeting between two or more people—often a memorable one!

**Futuristic**
Even more advanced than today's most modern ideas and things.

**Gruesome**
So horrible to look at it makes you feel uncomfortable—or unwell!

**Hollywood**
An area on the West Coast of the USA, where many movies are made.

**Hologram**
A set of light patterns that create the illusion of a real, solid object.

**Illusion**
Something that is not what it appears, like a magic trick or a hologram.

**Indestructible**
Impossible to break or destroy—a description things rarely live up to!

**Journalist**
Someone who writes or reports for newspapers, websites, and/or TV.

**Levitation**
Floating in the air without visible effort or support, as if by magic.

**Magpie**
A kind of bird, often black and white, that is said to like shiny objects.

**Multiverse**
A set of universes existing together without knowledge of each other.

**Quinjet**
A type of airplane made especially for S.H.I.E.L.D. and the Avengers.

**Radiation**
Invisible energy waves with many uses, including power generation.

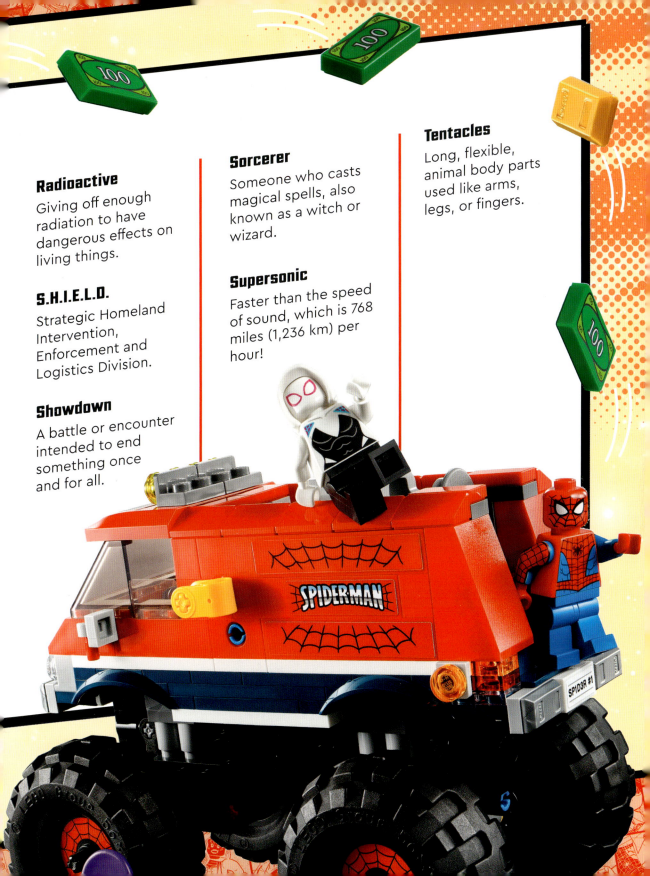

### Radioactive
Giving off enough radiation to have dangerous effects on living things.

### S.H.I.E.L.D.
Strategic Homeland Intervention, Enforcement and Logistics Division.

### Showdown
A battle or encounter intended to end something once and for all.

### Sorcerer
Someone who casts magical spells, also known as a witch or wizard.

### Supersonic
Faster than the speed of sound, which is 768 miles (1,236 km) per hour!

### Tentacles
Long, flexible, animal body parts used like arms, legs, or fingers.

# Index

**A**
Adrian Toomes 50–51
Aleksei Sytsevich 54–55
Amazing Spider-Man 37
Anya Corazon 30–31
Aunt May 12, 13, 32
Avengers 18–19, 50

**B**
Ben Reilly 32–33
Black Widow 18, 19

**C**
Captain America 18
Carnage 23, 26
Cloak of Levitation 35
cyborg suit 14

**D**
*Daily Bugle* 22–23
Daredevil 23
Doc Ock (Doctor Octopus) 22, 31, 37, 42–43
Doctor Strange 19, 35, 37

**E**
Electro 37, 49, 52–53

**F**
fire monster 47
Firestar 22
Flint Marko 48–49
Francine Frye 53
Friendly Neighborhood Spider-Man 37

**G**
Ghost-Spider 22, 28–29, 42
Green Goblin 20, 21, 22, 29, 36, 40–41
Gwen Stacy 12, 28–29

**H**
Harry Osborn 12

**I**
Iron Man 14, 18, 19, 50
Iron Spider suit 14–15

**J**
J. Jonah Jameson 22

**L**
Lizard 48

**M**
Mary Jane Watson 12
Max Dillon 52–53
Miguel O'Hara 34
Miles Morales 26–27, 44, 45
MJ 12, 37
monster truck 17, 42
Multiverse 34–37, 44
Mysterio 22, 46–47

**N**
Ned Leeds 12, 36
New York City 11
Norman Osborn 40–41

## O
Olivia Octavius  43
Oscorp  40

## P
Peter Parker  10–13
Pork Grind  44
Prime Spidey  36
pumpkin bombs  41

## Q
Quentin Beck  46
Quinjet  18–19

## R
Rhino  54–55

## S
Sandman  23, 48–49
Scarlet Spider  32–33
Scorpion  33

S.H.I.E.L.D.  26
Shocker  50, 51
Spider-Bike  20
spider-bots  21
Spider Crawler  16–17
Spider-Girl  30–31
Spider-Ham  35, 44
Spiderjet  17
Spider Lair  20–21
Spider-Man 2099  34
Spider-Man Noir  34
Spider-Man suits  14–15, 20
*Spider-Man: Far From Home* (movie)  47
spider-sense  21, 45
spider tattoo  30
Spider-Woman  29
Statue of Liberty  36
stealth suit  14

## T
Thor  18
Tony Stark  14, 50

## U
Uncle Ben  12, 32

## V
Venom  23, 44–45
venom blasts  27
Vulture  50–51

## W
webs  11, 14, 17, 31, 33

## Z
Zombie Hunter Spidey  35

**Senior Editor** Laura Palosuo
**Designers** James McKeag and Thelma-Jane Robb
**US Senior Editor** Jennette ElNaggar
**Senior Production Editor** Jennifer Murray
**Senior Production Controller** Lloyd Robertson
**Managing Editor** Tori Kosara
**Managing Art Editor** Jo Connor
**Publisher** Paula Reagan
**Art Director** Charlotte Coulais
**Managing Director** Mark Searle
**Jacket Designer** James McKeag

DK would like to thank Randi K. Sørensen, Heidi K. Jensen, and Martin Leighton Lindhardt at the LEGO Group; Chelsea Alon at Disney Publishing; Lauren Bisom and Farah Javed at Marvel Comics; Kristy Amornkul, Sarah Beers, Capri Ciulla, and Jacqueline Ryan-Rudolph at Marvel Studios; and, at DK, Julia March for proofreading and indexing, and Sophie Dryburgh for editorial assistance.

First American Edition, 2025
Published in the United States by DK Publishing,
a division of Penguin Random House LLC
1745 Broadway, 20th Floor, New York, NY 10019

Page design copyright © 2025 Dorling Kindersley Limited
25 26 27 28 29 10 9 8 7 6 5 4 3 2 1
001–344931–June/2025

LEGO, the LEGO logo, the Minifigure, and the Brick and Knob configurations are trademarks and/or copyrights of the LEGO Group.
© 2025 The LEGO Group. All rights reserved.

Manufactured by Dorling Kindersley, 20 Vauxhall Bridge Road, London SW1V 2SA, under license from the LEGO Group.

© 2025 MARVEL

All rights reserved.
Without limiting the rights under the copyright reserved above, no part of this publication may be reproduced, stored in or introduced into a retrieval system, or transmitted, in any form, or by any means (electronic, mechanical, photocopying, recording, or otherwise), without the prior written permission of the copyright owner.
Published in Great Britain by Dorling Kindersley Limited

A catalog record for this book
is available from the Library of Congress.
ISBN 978-0-5939-6570-2
Library ISBN 978-0-5939-6696-9

DK books are available at special discounts when purchased in bulk for sales promotions, premiums, fund-raising, or educational use.
For details, contact:
DK Publishing Special Markets, 1745 Broadway, 20th Floor, New York, NY 10019
SpecialSales@dk.com

Printed and bound in China

www.dk.com

MIX
Paper | Supporting responsible forestry
FSC™ C018179

This book was made with Forest Stewardship Council™ certified paper—one small step in DK's commitment to a sustainable future. Learn more at www.dk.com/uk/information/sustainability

Your opinion matters
Please scan this QR code to give feedback to help us enhance your future experiences